Dedicated to

John Moncrief

with love.

Sunny Davenport hated peas, but her father loved them.

One night they had a terrible fight. Sunny's father heaped peas onto her plate and Sunny refused to take a bite.

Her father fumed. He begged, pleaded, and finally shouted,

"EAT YOUR" PEAS !!!

Sunny threw a pea at her father instead.

Red faced and frazzled, he said, "Even if it takes all night, you will eat those peas!"

Then he rose, clearing the table with a pea stuck to his nose.

Sunny took a deep breathe. Staring sadly at her plate, she knew she would have to eat the rest.

Then she remembered...

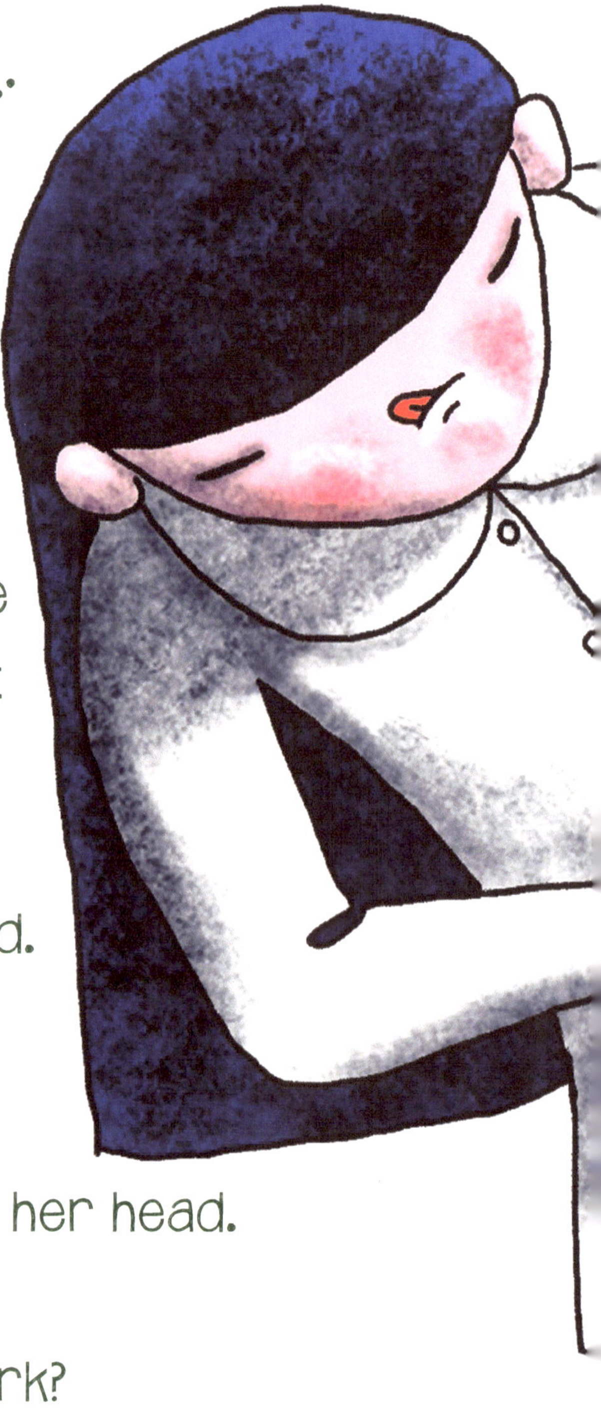

The pea she
had flung at
her father.
On his nose,
it had stayed.

A thought
popped into her head.

Would it work?

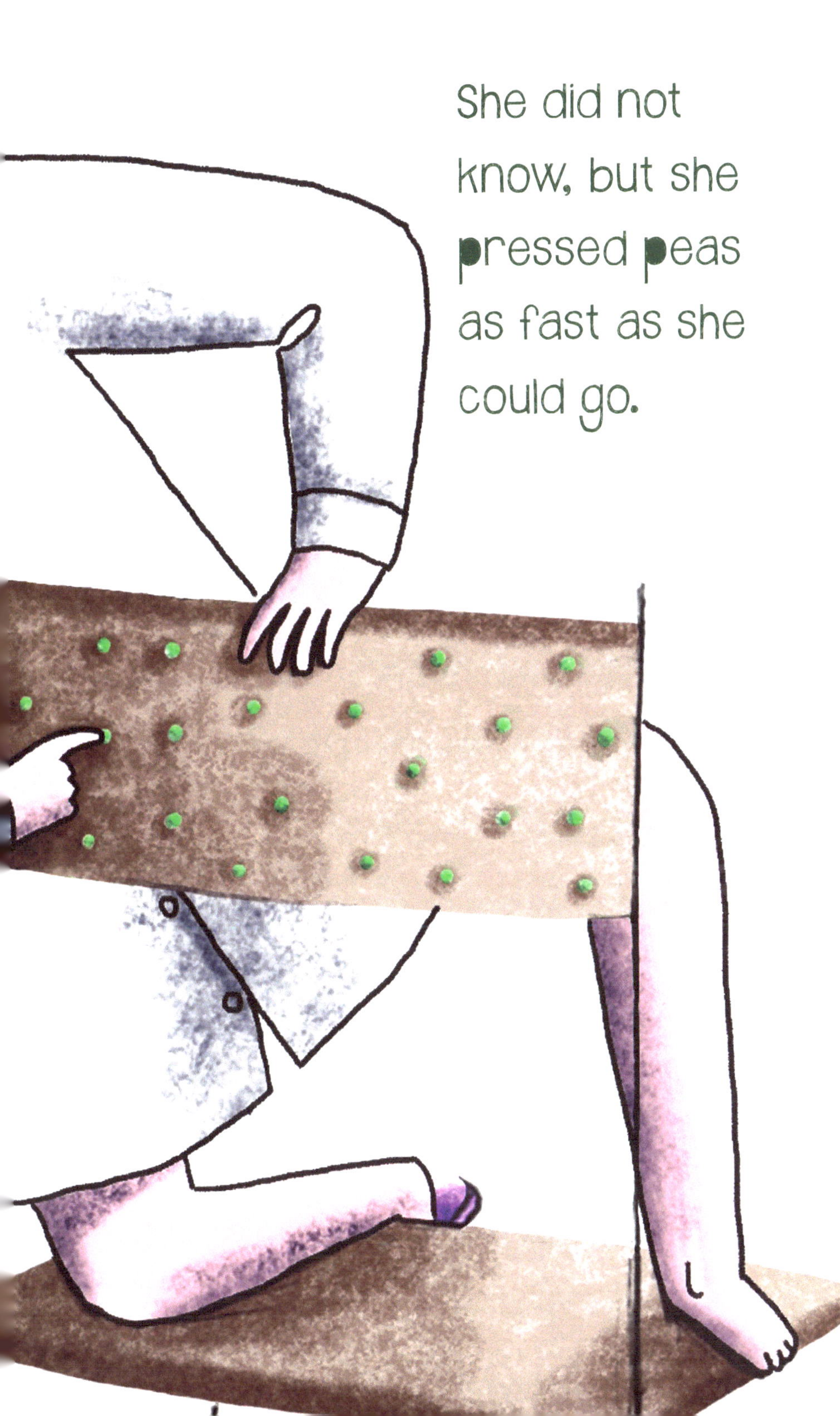
She did not know, but she pressed peas as fast as she could go.

Soon, the chair's backside was dotted green. Composed and calm,

Sunny's father came into the room. Sunny sat straight. She hoped those peas would stick.

As he came near, a bead of sweat dropped from her face and her little heart raced.

Proudly he smiled,

"Sunny you've done it!
You ate your peas!"

Sunny
sighed
with relief.

When he took her plate and left,
Sunny shoved those peas into her
pocket and ran to her room.

She called her friends and shared
the news.

"pressed peas
stick like glue!"

Word spread quick. Soon, no child
had to eat peas. Instead, when
the moment was right...

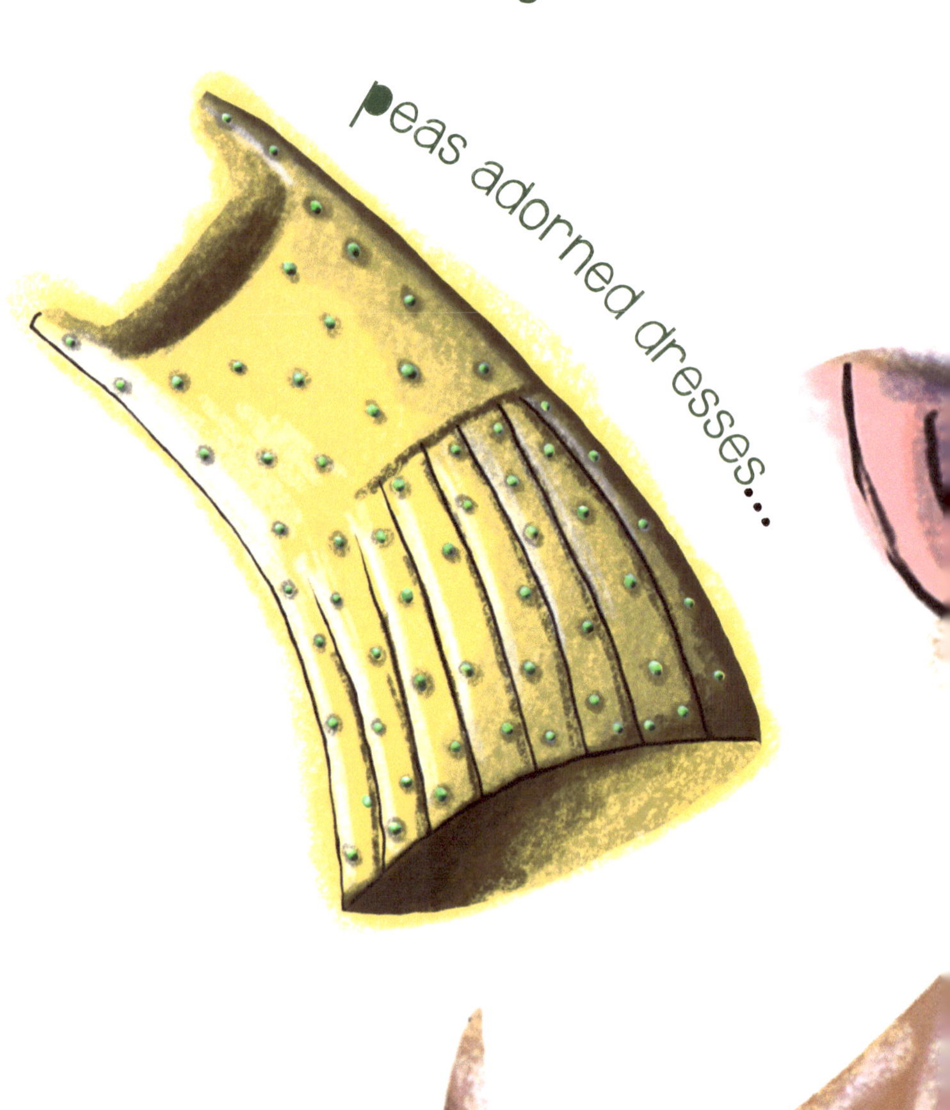

and the tops of shoes...

Even dog collars became perfect places for green pea glue.

All over town, children collected and hid their peas. They stashed them in...

dressers...

and drawers...

under beds...
and in pockets.

Mothers and fathers beamed,
as peas for dinner no longer
meant a fight.

Then one day, the children found a problem with their plan.

After months of squirreling, they had miles of piles of peas and nowhere left to hide.

Miles of piles of Peas!

Sunny called an emergency
meeting and the children gathered
close. They all thought hard...

Suddenly, Sunny had an
idea. She gleefully told
her friends,

"Next Saturday, bring
your peas and parents
too, down to the park
at noon!"

Over the next few days, every child had to confess. They revealed their stashes and hoped for the best.

Parents were not happy and some had to be begged, but on Saturday, every family arrived...

with wheelbarrows,

buckets,

boxes

and bags
filled with
peas.

Sunny greeted everyone and said, pile them high, we are going to have fun! Once every pea was stacked, she stepped to the podium, unrolled a banner and read,..

"Welcome to the first annual pea sculpting extravaganza!"

Sunny then declared,

"Let the sculpting begin!"

WELCOME
TO THE FIRST
ANNUAL PEA SCULPTING
EXTRAVAGANZA!

Parents looked confused and worried, but the children knew just what to do.

They dove into that mountain of peas and began making the most colossal creations. Soon...

two giraffes sat
on a park bench
sipping tea,

and a two-headed
dragon grew.

Followed by a
dancing narwhal
wearing a tutu.

With each inspired work the
children planned and sculpted.

Finally when the last pea had
been used, parents gathered
and deliberated.

A ribbon would go to the
"Best in Show."

Sunny stepped up to the winner with ribbon in hand,
when a sudden urge overtook her.
1st
WINNER

Sunny plucked a pea from the nose of the beast and bravely put it into her mouth. She savored it and everyone gasped.

With a knowing smile,
Sunny stated,

"Not bad, kind of tasty."
Not bad, kind of tasty!

What happened next was truly an amazing sight. Children dove in and devoured those crazy mixed-up creatures and ate every bite.

"Not bad, kind of tasty."

the children cheered,

"Not bad, kind of tasty!"

"Not bad, kind of tasty!"
"Not bad, kind of tasty!"

With her father by her side,
Sunny stepped to the podium
and declared the event
a great success.

Her father added, "We will do it
again next year!"

Then, with a big hug, he bent
down and whispered softly into
Sunny's ear,

"Broccoli is next, my dear."

"Broccoli is next, my dear."

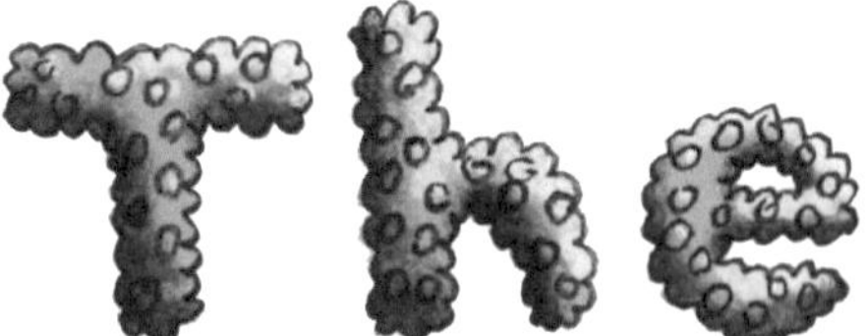

The